Let's go to the Balloons

A road-user education book
Roadwise Educational Publishers

Written by Jean Roberts
Illustrated by Colin Hale

Illustrated by Colin Hale

First published in Great Britain 2006 by
Roadwise Educational Publishers
P O Box 4555
Halesowen
B63 4SY
UK
www.5alive.org.uk

Text Copyright © Jean Roberts 2006
Illustrations Colin Hale
© Roadwise Educational Publishers 2006

British Cataloguing in Publication Data
A Catalogue record for this book is available from the British Library

Printed and bound in Great Britain by Goodman Baylis Ltd

ISBN 0 9524272 4 9

Early morning surprise

Whoosh......whoosh.

Sara peeped out from under the duvet.

"What's that?" she whispered to Rachel.

"I think aliens from Mars are landing," said

Rachel in a hushed voice.

"Aaagh!" shrieked Sara as she slid under the bedclothes.

"There it is again. I think they are landing in our garden," came a muffled voice from under the duvet.

Both girls suddenly sat up in their beds. There really was a loud noise outside their house. They crept to the window and nervously peeped through the curtains.

"It's the balloons!" The girls both shrieked with laughter and relieved not to see aliens in their back garden!

Quickly they ran to Adam's bedroom.

"Wake up!" they yelled as they shook his bed vigorously.

"Ugh, what's up, is the house on fire?"

mumbled Adam half asleep.

"It's the balloons," chorused the girls.

"It's not your birthday," replied Adam confused and still not really awake.

"No, no, not ordinary balloons, hot air balloons!" replied Rachel excitedly.

They all ran back into the girls' room, almost immediately joined by their parents, who'd been woken by the commotion.

"Whatever's going on?" asked their father, "it's only just after 6 o' clock."

"It's the balloons!" yelled Sara and Rachel.

"Listen," said Sara putting her finger to her lips.

Everyone went quiet.

Whoosh........whoosh.

They looked out of the window.

"There they are!" shouted Rachel.

There were as many as ten balloons: they filled the sky with exciting colours and shapes.

"They seem to be so near we can almost touch them," laughed Adam.

"Look – there are more coming this way. Let's go into the street so that we can have a better view," suggested their mother.

They put on their dressing gowns and clattered down the stairs. Their father tried to open the door quickly, but in his haste he fumbled with the key and both Rachel and Adam were beginning to get cross with him, which of course made it worse!

"Now just be quiet all of you, and then I shall be able to unlock the door," grunted their

6

father.

They found that their neighbours were already there, and even old Mrs McKenzie had struggled out on her two walking sticks to see the fun! It was like an early morning street party – dressing gown style! They waved to the people in the balloons and stood craning their necks skywards. The street was bustling with people and everyone was chatting happily, even those who didn't normally speak to one another!

"Doesn't the sky look pretty with all these balloons?" Mother was enchanted.

There were lots of traditionally shaped balloons, but some had rather exciting shapes: one like a squirrel and another looked as though someone was sitting in an armchair in the sky!

"Look at that one!" shouted Adam "it's shaped like a house!"

Balloon after balloon after balloon went over their heads and they watched for a long time until they had all vanished.

When they had disappeared Rachel dashed inside to find the local paper, hunting through it for any information about a balloon event; at last she found what she was looking for.

"The balloon festival takes place today and tomorrow at the common, and the balloons go up at 6am and 6pm, weather permitting," read Rachel. "So they will go up again this evening."

"Can we go and see them?" asked Adam.

"Yes, I should think so," replied Father, turning to Mother to see if she had anything else planned for then.

"That sounds a lovely idea," agreed Mother.

Although it was still very early, they all

decided to have breakfast and then go back to bed. The children read some of their comics and books as they were too excited to go back to sleep! It was not long before they were getting washed and dressed. Each of them had chores to complete: cleaning shoes, tidying their bedroom, helping with the dishes and any other jobs their mother and father might ask them to do, but today there was excitement in the air and, instead of grumbling or complaining, there was laughter as they worked!

All the fun of the fair!

Their parents had said that Adam's friend Ben could go with them if he were free. The family watched Adam as he spoke to Ben over the 'phone.

"Never! See you round here at about 3.30pm,"

replied Adam.

"And what was that all about?" asked Father.

"Ben says that there is one huge balloon called 'Mrs Stopcars' and if the weather is good enough it goes up into the air," replied Adam.

"Sounds as if we shall have a good time," Father answered.

"I can't wait," gasped Sara excitedly.

Ben arrived early and told them that the traffic was unusually heavy on the roads.

"We'd better not be long before we set off," said Adam thinking that they didn't want to miss anything.

"Make sure you put on some sensible shoes!" shouted Father from the kitchen.

"And a warm jumper," added Mother.

"But it's summer!" protested Sara.

"I know, dear, but we shall be standing around for a long time, and the common can be a cold place," explained Mother.

"I'm going to take my fold-up anorak," shouted Rachel, "and then I can wear it if I'm cold and I won't have to take a jumper as well."

Rachel could read her mother's mind: her mother never seemed to travel anywhere without taking clothes for the Arctic and the Mediterranean at the same time!

The common was only just over a mile from their house, so they decided to walk. It seemed as though everyone were going to watch the balloons, as cars were even parked on roads near their house.

At last they were all ready to go. They had no choice but to cross a road that had cars parked bumper to bumper and this presented them with a new problem.

"I've never seen so many cars in this road before," said Ben. "I think that people must have come from a long way away. This event is always very popular."

They would have to cross the road. Adam's Father took control of the situation: he told them to look for the safest place to cross the road. They looked up and down the road, but cars were bumper to bumper all the way. They decided that where they were was probably the safest place to cross the road as farther down the road was a junction.

They stood on the pavement near the kerb and kept looking and listening for traffic. They looked along the road and noticed several cars going past, presumably looking for a place to park.

"Check to see if there is a driver in the vehicles either side of you, as they might be about to move the vehicle." Adam's father indicated with his hands. "Look to see if any of the vehicles are about to move forwards or reverse. You can do this by checking to see that there aren't any lights shining, remember they are white and at the rear of the car.

Adam went quickly to the back of a car and was standing in the road looking around the car for a white light.

"Don't go into the road, Adam, and there is no need to bend down, stand up straight," shouted his father. "Stand on the pavement and look: you will see if a white light is on. If you go into the road and there is a driver who decides to reverse at the very moment you are bending searching for a light, he wouldn't be able to see you and so you could be knocked down."

Adam retraced his steps to the pavement.

"There's the light, but it isn't on," said Adam as he suddenly spotted the white light.

Ben had gone to the window of the car, put his hands either side of his face and peered in. "No driver here," he said.

"You don't need to peer into the vehicle *quite* so determinedly," laughed Adam's father. "If all is clear check the road before you leave the kerb to see if there are any cars or other vehicles travelling along the road."

They all looked this way and that along the road, cars were still moving past them.

Adam's father moved out between the cars and stood just short of the outside edge of the cars.

"Move out carefully between the cars and stop

just before you reach the outside edge of the vehicles," continued father.

Ben followed Adam's father, there was just enough room to stand beside him. Everyone else remained on the pavement.

"Wait where you are until the road is clear," said Father.

Ben waited and waited. When the road was clear Adam's father continued, "now look and listen again and if safe to do so, and yes it is, walk straight across the road, remembering to keep looking and listening as you cross the road, just in case anything unexpected happens."

"Well done," said Adam's father. "Now it's Adam's turn."

Adam, always in a rush, had to be told to stop and check the road when he was level with the parked cars. If his father hadn't been there to stop him, he would have gone straight into the road without waiting and checking to see that the road was clear. Adam felt a little foolish having to be reprimanded in front of his new friend Ben.

The road seemed to become quiet again and Adam kept looking and listening and, as the road was clear, he walked straight across the road, remembering to keep looking and listening as he crossed to the pavement on the other side.

"Well done, you got there safely in the end, but you must wait and check the road again when you are near the outside edge of the cars, it's the same as if you were on the pavement when crossing the road without cars parked," warned his father sternly.

Sara seemed to wait for ages just in from the outside edge of the parked cars, even though there were now no vehicles in sight! Her father, sensing her fear, encouraged her to cross the road when it was safe to do so. Father reminded Adam and Sara to keep looking and listening as they crossed the road, something they had been trained to do since they were very young, when walking across roads using Pelican and Zebra crossings.

When they were all safely on the pavement they continued walking along in the direction of the common. Ben and Adam were busy chatting. Ben had been many times to the balloon festival, and he was telling Adam all about it. For Adam's family it was their first visit to the balloon festival as they'd only recently moved to the town. Ben said that there was a fair right next to the balloons with lots of stalls, dodgem cars and rides. Rachel overheard them talking.

"I guess you'll want to test your throwing skills, Adam. You are always telling us how clever you are though we have never seen you win anything! I think I'd like to go on the big wheel. How about you Sara?" Rachel turned up her nose at her brother and then looked towards her sister.

"That sounds great," agreed Sara, "it all sounds

such fun."

"I'm sure we'll have a wonderful time," said father.

As they continued walking, more and more people joined them. They still had another road to cross, but this time there were double yellow lines on the road, so there weren't any parked cars!

"We'd better use the island in the middle to help us cross the road safely," announced Rachel.

"Yes," replied her mother, "the traffic is speeding past and besides, wherever we are we must always choose the safest place to cross the road, and that is at the island."

They walked along the road until they were opposite the island and stood on the pavement near the kerb. They kept looking and listening for traffic. Traffic was going past quickly in both directions, and they waited a long time before there was a lull in the traffic when they could cross to the island.

They checked the road again, and, as it was still clear, they began to walk straight across to the island.

"We need to keep looking and listening as we cross the road," Sara reminded everybody.

"Yes," said father, "just in case anything unexpected happens."

They reached the island and Adam soon got impatient waiting to cross the other half of the road. "We are having to wait ages to get across the road," said Adam almost ready to make a dash between the cars.

"Better to wait and get there, than be in a hurry and arrive somewhere else," said father, grabbing hold of Adam so that he could not dart out into the road.

"What do you mean?" questioned Ben.

"Well, it's better to wait until it's safe to cross the road than to dash across and maybe end up in hospital - or worse," explained Mother.

Ben thought about what Adam's mother had said. Just recently, when he was out with his friends Matthew and Steve, they had played a game daring each other to dash across the road and he remembered that once he'd been nearly hit by a car. He decided that he wouldn't ever

play with those friends near roads again, even

if they called him names. He wouldn't be

foolish and run across a road again; it was too dangerous.   He didn't want to end up in hospital - or worse.

"Come on, we can cross the road now," urged Mother, "and remember to keep looking and listening as you cross."
By now they could hear the noise of people and sounds of the fair.

"Just keep hold of your purses in your pockets as there will be a lot of people around. I know you haven't got much money on you, but you don't want it stolen," warned Father.
"Not far now," said Rachel, "but how will we cross the main road just before the common?"
"There's a subway," said Mother, "and we shall

use that."

"Oh yes, when we were little you told us that a subway was normally a good place to cross a very busy road as there aren't any cars to look out for," chuckled Rachel.

"Well, it still holds true even now that you are older," replied Mother.

As they approached the subway it was like school, with ten classes of children all trying to get through one set of double doors at the same time: there were swarms of people all being jostled by one another. They held on to their purses and all kept together, even though that was difficult at times.

As they emerged from the subway they could see lots of tents and sideshows – even more intriguing a massive area was roped off!

"It will be a while before the balloons go up so I suggest that we look around first," said Mother.

"We will need to get in a good position near to the rope so that we can see the balloons clearly," said Ben with an air of authority. "We need to be there in good time, before everyone else arrives."

"Yes, but I think we still have plenty of time to look around," replied Father.

"Oh look, there's the big wheel, we could see all the common from up there. Can we have a ride on it, please?" begged Rachel.

"What about you two boys, do you want to come?" asked Father.

"Bit slow for us I think," retorted Adam. "We'll go over to the more exciting rides!"

"What do you mean?" Rachel demanded, "going on the big wheel is exciting, and anyway, I was the one who survived that daring ride when we went to the theme park. Remember? It was you who turned a pale shade of green!"

"Enough of this!" said Father. "Mum, do you want to go with the girls and I'll go with the boys, and then we'll meet up again in half an hour back here?"

The boys went to the large star wheel that had cages at each of the points. Father said that he would watch them, but he didn't fancy going upside down and round and round at great speed! Their father could never understand how they could actually enjoy being thrown around; he said that he'd need to be paid to suffer such discomfort! Each of the boys was safely strapped in the seats, then they whirled round and round, up and down and their father even felt dizzy watching them!

Ben and Adam thought the ride was great! They sat down on the grass for a few minutes afterwards while their heads caught up with them! They weren't going to admit that they felt a bit giddy!

They spotted a stall where they had to throw a ball into an old fashioned milk churn.

"Here's your chance! Let's see how good you are Adam!" shouted Ben. "Here goes!" Ben had his go. His ball hit the side of the churn, but bounced off. He felt quite pleased with himself as he had very nearly scored. "Next time I'll get it in," smiled Ben contentedly.

Adam had several turns, but each time the ball

eluded the target, and never did go into the churn.

Adam began to get annoyed. "Huh," grimaced Adam as he had another go. Even Adam with all his pride failed to score.

"I'm not wasting any more money here," said Adam. "I'm off to the dodgem cars."

"Hey, wait for us!" called Adam's father as he took another unsuccessful aim at the churn.

That was their final throw - off they trooped - to the dodgem cars.

"I think Adam will go crashing into everything with the mood he's in," laughed Ben.

Adam's Father agreed. "There he is!"

It was easy to spot him with his red hair. He

often suffered from remarks about its colour; embarrassing him and causing him to lose his temper, especially when he got called names such as 'carrot top'.

Adam was already in a dodgem car and hurtling at great speed towards another car.

"Wait for the crash!" laughed Ben as he put his fingers to his ears.

It wasn't long before Adam's father and Ben were racing around and crashing into Adam. In a nice way they really seemed to be conspiring against him, managing to hit his car several times! Then Adam went on the attack towards both of them, hitting Ben head on.

They really enjoyed themselves and Adam was feeling more confident, he seemed to have

forgotten the 'unfriendly' milk churns.

"There they are!" shouted Adam. "I can see Rachel."

Rachel also had the same colour hair as Adam, and so it was easy to spot her in a crowd.

"Can we have a toffee apple, please?" asked Sara.

"Have you got enough money?" questioned her mother.

"Yes," replied Sara.

"Then off you go and get one," said mother. "Dad and I will wait here for you."

When they came back, Father suggested that it was probably time to go and get a good position by the rope.

"It's another half an hour until 6 o' clock," said Adam planning his next visit to one of the stalls.

"Well, let's go and get our place and then I will stay there and maybe Dad will go with you," said Mother.

After they had found a good place by a rope, Father, Ben and Adam hurried off back to the array of tents and sideshows.

It was 5.50pm when they got back to Mother and the girls. They had a struggle to get through the crowds, but finally they were there, in prime position, ready for the show!

Taking shape

A voice came over the loudspeaker system telling the pilots to report to a particular tent for last minute information.

"It must be getting near to lift-off," said Rachel, her eyes shimmering with excitement.

Soon people were running to their balloons and beginning to unroll them. Great care was taken to lay out the balloons so that there wouldn't be any problems when they began to inflate.

"My, what's this?" asked Ben puzzled. The balloon being unfolded right in front of them looked twice as long as the others.

"It's so long," said Sara, "I think it must be a special one."

Several people were involved in making sure that this enormous balloon was laid out correctly. Someone started to unroll parts going out to the sides of the main balloon.

"It looks as though this one has arms," laughed Sara.

"And look at this bulge right in front of us,"

said Ben, "I think it's a head."

"Then it must be the 'Mrs Stopcars' balloon," yelled Adam, jumping up and down with excitement. "To think that it is right in front of us."

"Well, we couldn't have had a better position could we?" said Father. "I think you're right, it is Mrs Stopcars."

They had heard over the loudspeakers that the Mrs Stopcars' balloon would be going up this afternoon, but actually to see it being inflated in front of their eyes was just amazing!

Some of the more traditionally shaped balloons were now partially inflated and jostling with each other for the available space.

"The balloons almost seem to have characters of their own," said Rachel. "Just look over there how the red balloon is determined to knock the green one out of the way and show who is boss!"

"Look at that one," shouted Ben, "it's the shape of a dodgem car."

"And there's one shaped like a house," giggled Sara. "Oh, and there's the man in the arm chair and the squirrel we saw this morning."

"Just look at all those bright balloons, yellow, green, red and multicoloured," said Mother, "they are just so pretty."

"They're at it again," said Rachel, "look at those three pushing each other. The one in the middle has little chance with those two 'I'm bigger than you' bullies swamping it."

Somehow all three balloons managed to fight for their space and were ready for lift off, but what was happening to 'Mrs Stopcars?'

The large balloon was being pulled into shape. "Mrs Stopcars looks a bit lifeless, doesn't she?" laughed Sara.

"I think they will inflate her now she has been laid out flat," said Mother.

Soon 'Mrs Stopcars's body was beginning to appear. It kept swelling and swelling. People were helping with her head and arms to make sure they inflated correctly!

"We can't see anything now except her enormous head and hat," laughed Ben. "We can even touch it as it is right here in front of us."

All their eyes now turned upwards as Mrs Stopcars's head was many metres high. It was huge!

"Up she goes!" shouted Adam jumping in the air with delight.

Mrs Stopcars's hat looked as though it were pushing against the ground and helping Mrs Stopcars to stand up straight. Mrs Stopcars kept her head facing the ground as she began to rise slowly.

Then there was Mrs Stopcars, completely upright, proudly holding up her head and with her arms and hands waving gently in the air.

"Isn't she magnificent?" gasped Sara as she put her hands to her mouth in amazement.

"Just look at the lollipop stick she has in one hand with the other hand moving as though she is stopping the traffic," gasped Ben.

"But why have a lollipop lady?" questioned Sara.

Mother explained that many of the balloons were advertising different products, for example, mobile phones, crisps, chewing gum, and drinks to name but a few. She said that she recalled having heard about a special road-user campaign in schools, and that the government had sponsored the Mrs Stopcars balloon to attract attention to the campaign. It had been named Mrs Stopcars as a Lollipop person wasn't thought to be such an exciting name.

"I don't think that our school knows about the campaign," remarked Ben, "but they very soon will. I shall tell them about the Mrs Stopcars balloon!"

"Mrs Stopcars is enormous!" observed Adam, "she is just so much taller than all the other balloons."

"I can't wait to see her go up into the sky," said Rachel.

"Neither can I!" chorused the others.

Into the air

The first balloons were rising gently into the sky. They kept hearing the 'whooshing' sound of the burners; in fact there was quite a noise from so many balloons being inflated and sounds of the fairground in the background.

"They're throwing something out of the basket!" shouted Ben.

"Perhaps the people are too heavy and they need to get rid of some weight," chortled Adam, not even bothering to look.

"I think they are sweets," said Rachel.

On hearing that Adam spun around and looked to see what was happening; then he began to scurry off in the direction of the sweets. Ben, Sara and Rachel followed him.

"Found one!" shouted Adam gleefully. He may not have succeeded with the milk churn but he was the first to find a packet of sweets and he was very pleased with himself.

The others looked on the ground but didn't

find any sweets. Suddenly Rachel had the bright idea of looking upwards to see if she could see them falling from the baskets of the balloons. This turned out to be a good idea as they spotted sweets coming down a little farther away from where they were. They ran over to the spot, only to find lots of other children also searching for sweets. They kept shouting out as they each found a packet.

A small child sat crying. They asked her what was the matter and she told them that she hadn't found any sweets so they asked her to come with them and look. There were so many children there, but Adam was quick to spot a packet of sweets that had been missed by others and called to the little girl.

She found the sweets and the beaming smile on her face was a satisfying reward for helping her.

She thanked them and went skipping away back to her parents.

"We'd better go back and see how Mrs Stopcars is getting on," said Adam still stuffing his mouth with sweets.

"Anyone would think you hadn't eaten for days the way you keep stuffing sweets into your mouth," said Rachel, disgusted at the way her brother was behaving.

They waved to the people in the balloons as they gently rose above the trees and higher into the sky.

"Hey, it looks as though Mrs Stopcars is about to go up!" shouted Sara. "Let's run back quickly to Mum and Dad."

They darted through the spaces in the crowd, but, as they got nearer to their parents, the crowd was more dense and they felt as though they were in a jungle as they battled their way past babies in buggies, toddlers trying to escape from their parents, and grown-ups who seemed to move slowly in every direction, so getting in the children's way. Finally they made it.

"We've just about managed to keep you a space," said Father. "Everyone wants to see Mrs Stopcars go into the air, and we are probably in the best position."

"We've made it just in time," sighed Sara with relief, her eyes fixed on Mrs Stopcars.

"You have to be a very experienced pilot to fly

Mrs Stopcars," said Father, "because it is a very difficult balloon to control."

"A very special pilot for a very special person," said Sara.

Their necks began to feel the strain as Mrs Stopcars rose up into the sky.

Everyone clapped as Mrs Stopcars rose gently and smoothly upwards. It certainly was a very large balloon.

"Look, she's winking at us," laughed Sara pointing at Mrs Stopcars.

"Oh yes," shouted Ben, "I think she knows we didn't expect to see her here!"

"Yes, she certainly seems to be laughing at us here on the ground!" remarked Mother.

The balloon moved slowly away in the direction of the trees.

"Mrs Stopcars balloon is dropping sweets too," exclaimed Adam and again he hurried off.

"These are shaped like Mrs Stopcars!" laughed Sara as she picked up a foil covered chocolate.

There were lots of children hunting for sweets one minute and then craning their necks to watch Mrs Stopcars, who was now right above them. The mass of balloons looked so pretty against the background of the clear blue sky.

By now there must have been nearly a hundred balloons in the sky and Mrs Stopcars rose higher and higher. They gazed upwards unable to take their eyes off her.

"I wonder where they will travel to?" said Sara wishing she were with them on their journey, and especially in Mrs Stopcars' balloon!

Life after the balloons

"Can we have some popcorn?" asked Sara.

"I'd rather have an ice cream," argued Adam.

"Well, let's go over to the food area and we can each choose what we want," said Mother.

When they got to the food area there was

such a choice, from ice creams to take-away meals.

Mother said that they would have a meal when they got home, so even if they wanted a 'take away,' the children realised that it was no use arguing with Mother, they would have to settle for an ice cream or some other light snack.

"There's an ice lolly in the shape of Mrs Stopcars," said Rachel pointing to a giant size lollipop.

"Then I'd like one of those," said Adam.

"So would I!" replied the others.

"Don't you want popcorn Sara?" asked Mum, knowing Sara's weakness for popcorn.

"No thanks. These Mrs Stopcars look much more exciting," replied Sara.

"Mrs Stopcars' for all," said Dad as he spoke to the person selling them. "That's six in all please."

The wrapper around the lollipop had a message for everyone telling people to always look for the safest place to cross a road, which could be a footbridge, subway, Pelican, Zebra or lollipop person, for example; to walk to it and wait on the pavement looking and listening for traffic. When safe to do so, walk straight across the road remembering always to keep looking and listening as they cross a road (just in case anything unexpected happens).

"This Mrs Stopcars is yummy," said Ben as he licked his lollipop.

"Every Mrs Stopcars is nice," said Sara, "the ice lolly, all Lollipop persons and of course the balloon! They all want us to be safe as we cross a road."

"I wonder where the Mrs Stopcars balloon is now?" queried Father.

"Far, far away," replied Sara dreamily, picturing Mrs Stopcars ordering the cars to stop, as she floated along in the sky with her lollipop pole in one hand and her other hand outstretched.

All the balloons had now taken to the sky. They watched, straining their necks, right until the last one became just a small speck.

"We can all have a quick visit to the fair

before we go home," said Mother looking at her watch.

"Great!" said Adam ready to go off to the dodgems again.

Ben was keen to join Adam, and mother decided to go with the boys this time, while father and the girls would have a wander round the stalls, and then join the others at the dodgems.

"Oh, here are tee shirts with a Mrs Stopcars design on them." said Rachel, "and they have another road crossing on the back. Can I have one please?"

"I'll pay for it now, but it will have to come out of your pocket money," said her father.

There were all sorts of things to buy: pencil cases, pencils in the shape of Belisha

Beacons, rulers, rubbers, badges and lots of

other things. There were books for younger children, skills and activity books and crossing roads safely when abroad. One was even written partly in French! Father focused his attention on the books for younger children.

"I think I'll buy two of these 'On the Way' books for your younger cousin Daniel as it's his birthday very soon," said Father. "I think he would enjoy them and they may help him to cross a road safely."

"There's a CD of a song to go with the books," said Rachel. "We could buy that for Daniel's birthday too."

"What a lovely idea. You children buy the CD and Mum and I will buy Daniel the books. Now....which books shall we buy?" wondered Father.

They looked at each of the books carefully before making their choice.

"I'll buy you each one of these books. Look, there are lots of activities to do," said Father.

"Hey, they look great. There are certificates to get too," replied Rachel. "Thanks Dad."

When they had paid for the books and CD

they were handed a leaflet giving details about a competition to win a mountain bicycle, cycle helmet, road-user education books, and much, much more. They were also given bookmarks giving guidelines of how to be safe when crossing roads. The competition form had to be handed in to a teacher at school so they decided to complete it when they got home.

"I'd still like to buy one of those brightly coloured tee shirts. Let's see how much they are," said Rachel.

The price seemed good value and Sara and Rachel decided to buy one each.

"We shall be reminded of a really super day with Mrs Stopcars every time we wear them," said Sara.

"I'm going to buy a green one," said Rachel.

"And I'll have a yellow one," replied Sara.

Of course, when the boys saw what Sara and Rachel had bought they were off to buy a tee shirt too. However, when they got there they rather liked the pencils. They were cheaper than the tee shirts and, as neither of them ever had much money to spare, they decided to be different from the girls and buy a large pencil.

"Look what Dad has bought each of us," said Rachel as she handed the books to Adam and Ben.

"Wow, they look super, and we can get certificates too," replied Adam.

"Well, Ben may get them, but I think you'll

have to improve a lot before you would get one!" Rachel sniggered.

"I think Adam would work hard and learn fast," replied his good friend Ben.

"Let's hope so," said Mother.

"I've got just enough money for one last go at the milk churn," said Adam.

"But you know what happened last time," warned Father.

"Ah, but that was last time and I'm sure I shall win this time," replied Adam confidently.

"That's where your money goes, on things that don't give good returns," said Father shaking his head.

Adam shot off and they all wearily followed him. They sensed what would happen; Adam wouldn't win and he would be in a bad mood.

They watched Adam as he had his turn. He hit the milk churn, but as before, the ball failed to go into the churn.

It was a disappointed Adam who left that stall. He was convinced he should have won a prize.

"Come on Adam, cheer up!" said Ben.

As they were making their way to the subway they passed a stall advertising exotic fruit. Outside there were cars in the shape of an orange, a coconut and a pineapple.

"Oh how I'd love to drive one of those!" said Adam already picturing himself in the driving seat.

"Oh yes," gasped Ben also itching to have a go.

"Come and drive me," called a voice. Adam and Ben looked around. The voice came again. "Come and drive me." Adam and Ben sped off in the direction of the sound. There, inside a large van were replicas of the cars outside. Inside the cars were simulators so that people could climb inside and 'drive'. They each chose a 'fruit' car, stepped inside, connected onto the controls and off they went, driving along a road!

Adam soon came to a sticky end! Up on the screen came the message 'driving is a skill that needs to be learnt well. We advise you to get Driverwise, and so become competent on the road.' Ben, who was always much more placid than Adam was given, 'well tried, with care and training you could become a competent driver.' Sara was told to have more confidence and not to hesitate so much. Rachel was given 'well done' and like Ben was encouraged that she too, with training would be welcomed as a driver on the roads. As for mother and father, they were given a few tips to improve their driving skills. All of them like Adam, were advised to attend Driverwise at the National Road User Activity Centre and were offered a leaflet about it.

"I wish real cars were fruit shaped. I can see myself driving around in the latest coconut model," squealed Rachel.

"One with sunglasses on," laughed Ben.

"And with a head that turns to look at people," said Adam.

"A head with expression and movement!" giggled Rachel.

They went outside again and stood admiring the cars before continuing their journey home.

"Straight through the subway, and I hope it won't be so crowded," said Adam in a voice that sounded as though he was in charge of an army leading his troops into battle.

The other main road was a little quieter than when they had crossed it before, but they were still several minutes standing on the pavement before there was a gap in the traffic.

"Why do we look like people watching a tennis match?" asked Ben.

"I don't know," said Adam, "why?"

"Because we keep moving our heads from side to side like watching a tennis ball going across the net," said Ben.

"Come on," said father, "it's safe for us to cross the road now."

"And remember to keep looking and listening as we cross the road," said Rachel, "only it's not tennis balls we're looking for, but cars, bicycles, and people who could cause us to change direction in some way."

They crossed the first half of the road and were waiting on the island in the middle.

"Wait, I can hear something," remarked

Sara.

Sure enough, within a few seconds the sound of a siren could be heard loudly.

"Keep yourselves well back from the road!" shouted father as the noise of the siren became deafening.

"That was a bit close," squealed Ben, "there

wasn't much room on the island to move back as we would have been in the way of traffic from the other side. It could have been dangerous if there had been a crowd of people as there was when we came."

"It just shows how important it is always to keep your own space and to keep away from the road," said father. "If you are in a crowd and there isn't enough space on the island, remain on the pavement, don't just follow everyone else and hope that you'll be safe."

They were all a little shaken, but still remembered to keep looking and listening as they crossed the road. Soon they were almost home and there was only one road to cross before reaching their own house.

"Just look at all these parked cars," said Adam. "The road is still full of cars bumper to bumper!"

"I expect they belong to people who also went to see the balloons," replied Mother. "It's obviously a very popular event."

"Yes, and to think we might have missed it if we hadn't been woken by the balloons this morning," said Rachel smiling.

"Now we can again practise crossing a road where there are parked cars," said father. "Rachel, you tell us what to do please."

"Look for the safest place to cross the road and walk to it," said Rachel confidently.

They looked along the road.

"I think that if we walk to the white car we

shall have a clearer view of the road as there is a little more space between it and the next car," said Ben.

They looked around and agreed that Ben had chosen a good place.

"Now look at the cars near you to make sure there isn't a driver or person in the vehicles," said Rachel.

"Checking that they aren't going to reverse or move forward," interrupted Sara.

"How can you know if they are reversing?" asked father.

"You can look to see if a white light is shining at the back of the car," replied Sara.

"Well done, Rachel and Sara! Now remember to look and see if there are any vehicles travelling along the road. Now Ben, you continue please," said father.

"If there is no driver or reversing light visible, you can move out carefully into the road between the parked cars. You stand up straight, and continue until you are almost level with the outside edge of the parked cars," said Ben.

"Excellent," said Dad, "and now Adam."

"Stand there and keep looking and listening for traffic. Wait until the road is clear."

"Well done," responded father, "and now back to Ben."

"When the road is clear look and listen again and if it is safe to do so walk straight across the road," answered Ben.

"Remembering to do what, Adam?" asked father.

"To keep looking and listening as you go across the road, just in case anything unexpected happens," Adam replied.

"I'm very impressed with all of you," said father, "and every time you cross a road if you do what you've just said, you should always arrive safely on the other side. Let's put it into practice now."

Aunt Jess and Uncle Ted

"I wonder if the balloons will come over our house again tomorrow?" chuckled Adam.

"We'll have to wait and see," said mother, "but now we need to have tea and get ready to go to Aunt Jess's and Uncle Ted's tomorrow."

"Oh yes that's right," remarked father, "with all the excitement of the balloons I had quite forgotten!"

Next morning there was no 'whooshing' sound to waken them so the children slept until Father woke them. The children spent the morning drawing pictures of the balloons they'd seen as they thought they would make a scrapbook reminding them of their special day. Then they filled in the competition form, by answering the questions and coloured in the Mrs Stopcars balloon.

After lunch they got in the car and headed off to the farm. The children always looked forward to visiting their aunt and uncle as they found them friendly and fun to be with, they were grown-ups that really appreciated children. They had four children and both families enjoyed playing their favourite game. It wasn't cricket and it wasn't rounders, but it was a good game: they knew it as 'Crocker' and played it in one of the fields; then afterwards there would always be a lovely tea with lots of homemade cakes and ice cream.

The weather was again fine, similar to the day before. When they arrived their aunt and uncle came out to greet them.

Everyone was excited at the thought of playing Crocker. There were two stumps about the width of a football apart and a bowler's stump about seven strides away. The other stump was to the left of the batman's stumps. The game was played with a soft volleyball and a plastic softball bat. The bowler had to bowl underarm and if the batter hit it, or it glanced off his or her bat then the batsman had to run around the stump to their left. The bowler could bowl the ball and try to hit the stumps even if the batsman had not got back to the wicket. Each player kept their own score and everyone else fielded, so everybody was on the go all the time!

Sometimes each family would add their score together and that was how they played it today. Richard and Emma were really good

at the game although Adam and his sisters

could play quite well and often managed to

overpower their cousins, aunt and uncle. Their secret was to keep aiming the ball away from Richard and Emma. However, today they couldn't quite get the ball to go where they really wanted it to, and Richard or Emma always seemed to be there to retrieve it!

"A clear victory for the Downtons," said Adam's father.

"That makes a change," said their aunt. "It's often the Robinsons who win!"

They pulled up the stumps and walked towards the farmhouse for tea. The table was laden with home-cooked pies, cakes and buns.

"It's a great spread," said Adam with his eyes

nearly popping out of his head.

"I'm glad it looks good and I hope you all enjoy it," replied aunt Jess feeling very happy.

Everyone enjoyed the wonderful tea, and not a crumb was left on anyone's plate.

Just as they finished eating there was a sudden 'whoosh' sound.

"I don't believe it!" yelled Adam as he sped off outside. Rachel followed close on his heels.

"It's the balloons!" shouted an excited Sara.

Everyone rushed outside.

There were several balloons in the sky and they waved to the people in them.

"They're coming down!" shouted Richard.

"I think it will be in those fields over there," said uncle Ted. "Come on everyone, let's go and greet them!"

Everyone was excited, but especially Adam, Sara and Rachel. Yesterday they had seen the balloons go up and now they were going to see them land!

Cars and trailers were driving into the field. "What's happening now?" asked Adam. "Who are all these people coming into your fields, uncle Ted?"

"They have been following the balloons and will help to put everything inside the trailer," replied their uncle.

"Remember the balloon will take a lot of space and may bump along the ground before coming to a stop and then the balloon itself will spread out over a large area," said their uncle, as he and the others ran towards the far field. "We'll wait here. We need to keep our distance from the balloons."

"There's one landing now," said Sara. "Oh, it's going up again, - no, it's just bumping along the ground. Now it's stopping."

It was so exciting. The sky seemed to be full of balloons, some coming down and some landing, and some being carefully folded and put into trailers.

"I wish I had my camera," said Adam. "Next time I visit I'll bring a camera just in case!"

"We'll have to draw some more pictures for our scrapbook," said Sara.

They spent a long time watching the balloons

land. Uncle Ted went over to speak to some of the balloonists. They were grateful that the field did not have any crops growing, as they didn't want to cause any damage.

One of the balloonists came over.

"I hear that you watched us go up yesterday," said one of the pilots speaking to Adam and his sisters.

"Yes, and we saw Mrs Stopcars being inflated and then rising into the sky," said Rachel.

"And we got some of the sweets which were thrown out," said Adam, always thinking of his stomach.

Rachel gave Adam's arm a rather hard nudge.

"So what would you say to having a flight in

a balloon?" asked the pilot.

"Wow, er do you mean it.....um, I mean, could we really?" spluttered Rachel completely amazed.

"Yes, here's my card and telephone number. We'll arrange for all of you to have a flight," said the pilot. "Invite some of your friends. We can take up to twelve people in one of our balloons."

"Thank you...thank you very, very much," stammered Adam.

"It's a pleasure. Thanks again, Ted, for letting us land in your fields," said the pilot. The pilot waved goodbye as he walked towards the balloon.

"Do you mean that we can really go up in a balloon?" asked Adam, unable to believe

what he had heard.

"Yes. Danny is a good friend and I thought he might be willing to give you a flight," said uncle Ted.

"Thanks, thank you so much, Uncle," said Sara running to give her uncle a big hug.

It was an excited and rather stunned group that arrived back at the farmhouse.

"I think I'd better put the kettle on," said their aunt. "Who's for a cup of tea and who wants a cold drink? Oh yes, and I think we'd better have some more cakes to celebrate!"

"What a wonderful day," said Rachel dreamily.

"What a fantastic two days!" agreed a rather excited Adam, who began to tell everyone yet

again about their adventures of yesterday,
seeing Mrs Stopcars inflated and then rising
majestically into the sky, ...not forgetting the
sweets!

"I look forward to seeing your scrapbook,"
said their aunt.

"We'll bring it to show you next time we come," said Adam.

"Thanks for a lovely day," said Sara.

"Yes, thank you very much," echoed Adam and Rachel.

They had had a wonderful time. They talked about what they would put into their scrapbook, they had a lot to write about and draw, and then they had the balloon flight to look forward to! Whom would they invite to join them on their flight? They were going to be busy!

Roadwise Educational Publishers exists to teach and encourage pedestrians (especially children) to make wise choices of where to cross a road and how to cross a road safely being aware and alert of the unexpected.

This book is based on 5 alive, (the Road Ed Code for crossing the road). 5 alive is fully explained (how to use hand to remember code) in the 5 alive Skills and Activity Books.

For more information log on to:
www.5alive.org.uk

Jean Roberts first became concerned about accidents to children on the road when a friend's daughter was killed. So, in memory of Helen, and to all children and everyone reading this book we hope that you will be safe when crossing a road.

Thank you to everyone who has been involved in the production of this book, the children, schools and numerous individuals.

Other books in the series:

Let's go to the carnival
Let's go to the Road-user Activity Centre

5 alive Skills and Activity Books 1-6 include a
wide range of activities including making,
learning, sorting, research, designing, writing,
colouring and working for awards and
proficiency certificates.

Log on to
www.5alive.org.uk
for more information